"I Love You"

is an interesting way to say goodbye

Molly Murray

BookLeaf Publishing

India | USA | UK

Made with ❤ on the BookLeaf Publishing Platform
www.bookleafpub.in
www.bookleafpub.com

Dedication

Poets write of nature, beauty, love, and heartbreak.

No one considers inviting the poet to the party to liven
things up.
Invite the musician,
invite the drunk,
the one who insists on karaoke...
but you invite me.

Terrible plan
but here we are.

This one is for you,
is about you.

Preface

Over breakfast, he asked
Do I still write poetry?
"I do," I replied.
With no follow-up or explanation.

Poetry is emotions
attempting to be expressed in words
that jumble around until the letters make feelings
and colour the page with ink made of tears.

Not all of them are lovely.
Some I've started
but never finished.
Because -
someday you may read them.

Turning the unspoken
into something tangible.

Acknowledgements

When the conversation turns to
happy memories,
fun times,
traditions,
and perfect days...

My happy memories are so often
edged with sadness.
What was and is no longer,
what never was at all.

I prefer to enjoy the right now
or to look into the future,
and find excitement there.

So my acknowledgment
is for those
who lifted me up
and those
who left me alone.

Every path
lead me straight to here.

1. January - The Mist

Hold my hand while I walk the path,
for it is misty, and I cannot see.
There may be warning signs missed
or dangers lurking.
But I trust,
that you will keep me
from wandering alone.

I'll hold your hand
for it is misty, and you cannot see.
There may be loose rocks
or roots that cause you to stumble.
But trust,
that I will keep you
from falling over the ledge.

2. February - Physical Poetry

He doesn't write poetry
he says.
Yet when together,
whispers all the words I need to hear.

Kissing his poetry on my neck
as the sun shines through the window
illuminating our bodies.

These moments,
reminding each other of who we are
and who we want to be.

Physical poetry
that is so much more
than words on paper.

3. March - Beautiful Dying

Flowers given in love
"I was thinking of you"
a "welcome home"
an "I missed you"
bought in anticipation of a return.

Kept in the window
the leaves start to dry around the edges
curling slowly inward.
The tips of the petals growing dark.

The flower hangs sleepy
pulling water from its stem
but too tired to remain bright.

Instead, just barely
hanging onto life.

It is in-between the world of the living and the dead.
A different kind of beauty.

It fades
requiring gentle care.
No longer able to sustain itself
no amount of tenderness will revive it.
Vulnerable
but no less beautiful.

Preserved love
but fragile.

4. April - Peace My Love

Peace, my love,
be still your heart in mine.
Loosen your furrowed brow,
and allow yourself to be loved,
to be cared for.

You deserve love.
Gentle care
in words,
in touch,
in deeds.

Let the love you give,
and the love you receive
speak of who you are.

It is enough.

5. May - Birch Trees

Birch trees
with green leaves just budding,
welcoming the return of warmth.

As snowflakes
drift down
covering them in the soft glow of afternoon light.

I watch the snow sweep over the trees in the gentle
breeze.

and I wait
for you to come back to me.

You are with someone else,
in another place
another time.

Separated from me
while we lie next to each other.

I wait for your return
while I marvel

at May snow
on birch trees.

6. June - Broken

Sometimes,
you come to me
broken
and defeated.
You come not for comfort
but for a moment to breathe
and allow yourself to be broken in my arms.

Sometimes,
I come to you
broken
sad and alone.
I come to you
not for comfort
but for a moment to breathe.
And allow myself to be vulnerable in your arms.

You see all of me.
I see all of you.

We can lay here

and hold each other
until we can breathe again.

7. July - Walkabout

No one knows
what stories will be told of them
after they are gone.

Stories of love,
of sorrow.
Grievances never to be rectified.
Adventures taken.

If the story you tell of me is one of a brief
but happy time

One in which I helped you
to refind yourself.

Then there are worst stories to be
in someone's life.

8. August - The Book

Found
not intended for you
but it was waiting for you nevertheless.

The person who it was meant for
left it to gather dust
on the back of the shelf.
Forgotten.

Until it was ready
to be found again
for the person
it was always predestined for.

9. November - Handwritten Letters

I didn't read the letter you wrote,
afraid that it was a goodbye.
I knew,
I couldn't read that.

Afraid
these might be the last words I heard from you.

So I waited
and had things gone differently,
perhaps I would have never opened the envelope at all.

Because
if you never say goodbye
then you are still with me.

10. December - Remember Forever

Remember Forever
when you couldn't help
but kiss me.

Remember Forever
sharing secrets,
fantasies,
and fears.

Remember Forever
the light coming through the window
at just the right angle.
The white sheets covering us
no longer two people.

Remember Forever
when we said goodbye in the doorway
not knowing if it would be the last time.
Aching for something we couldn't name.

Remember Forever
the perfect fall day
and a soft patch of grass.

Remember Forever
looking through the hoarfrost prismed window
at the dawning
of a new year.

Remember Forever
me sitting in the recovery room waiting for you
and you sitting in the recovery room
waiting for me.

Remember Forever
clouds
that covered only half the sky.

Remember Forever
tangoing in cowboy boots
and two-stepping on the sidewalk.

Remember Forever
when I saw all of you
And words didn't need to be spoken
and kisses expressed poetry.

when tears were licked off faces
and laughter was found in the oddest places.

Remember Forever
that I love you.

11. January "I love you" is an interesting way to say goodbye.

There are moments,
when your eyes
say goodbye.

Tears join the laughter
afraid that it might not last.

But "I love you"
is an interesting way to say goodbye.
Bitter and sweet
in equal measure.

Unwilling
unable
to let go.
but feeling like sand,
slipping between your fingers.

Wishing it had all gone differently
but knowing you would have missed
being right here,
right now,
if it had.

Each new moment of joy
rimmed with sadness
of things that won't ever be the same.
If only...
or what if...

Saying goodbye never feels like "I love you"

but sometimes,

"I love you"
sounds like goodbye.

12. March - Threads

A string
looping lazily through town.
Down paths and over creeks,
slipping under my door.
Reaching to connect your heart with mine.

Tugging at 3 a.m.

Pulling each other awake.

13. September - Photos

I didn't understand
why you took so many photos.

There is something there
that I can't always see.

More than the moment
or the image itself.

Inspired by beauty
or emotions
that must be captured.

For fear
that without them
someday,
you'll forget
and be lost
alone
not knowing if you had ever lived.

14. November - Names

Words have power
names more so.

How beautiful
or hurtful it can be
to hear your name
spoken from the lips of those you love.

15. January - Home

"Come home" you said.

How can two words
have so much meaning in them?

16. February - Twelve Dozen Roses

Twelve rose quarts
tied in elk hide that came from your grandfather.
Held together with a trade bead.
That lived with you
on your bag
for so many years.

Carried from place to place
as you moved through the world.
Providing protection and luck,
reminding you of the roots that tie you to that place and
time.

Every individual piece
filled with meaning and memories.
Weaving me into your history
with 12 dozen roses
that will last forever.

17. March - Following Footsteps

There is something comforting
that in a place you can never take me
knowing that I'm walking along the roads,
you once walked.

Inhaling the scent of the ocean
and seeing the light glint off the water.

In the same way, you experienced them.

In a way,
we now share this place
as much as we ever will.

18. April - Sometimes, I Need The Reminder

I wrap myself in you
most nights.
In clothes that linger
with your scent.

Sometimes, I forget.

I don't forget

Sometimes I don't
feel deserving
and I sleep in my clothes instead.

But when I remember
waking up to you
saying I'm beautiful...

I wrap myself in pieces of you
to remind myself.

19. September - Friends

Once,
I had a friend
who couldn't help but fall in love.

Love is most often
Unexpected
and
Inconvenient

Rarely does it find you
at the right time
or the right place.

Instead turning everything
upsidedown and sideways
leaving it difficult to breathe.

20. October - Lovers of words

As someone who is a lover of words
reading them
writing them
experiencing them spoken.

There is something
about the way we can speak
for minutes
or hours
with looks that can never fully be expressed
in a written form.

Eyes speak more than the most tender words.
The conversations they hold come from a place
that cannot be deceptive or hold back their meaning.

For two people
who talk as much as we do,
never lacking in something to say.

Spinning off of each other
moving quickly from one topic
sliding into the next.

Joining together conversations and moments of time
weaving them together to tell the story.

Rarely is there silence.
When there is,
we still talk.

Entire conversations had with looks.
Sharing of
love, desperation, grief, care, understanding, joy
filling these silent moments
with exchanges
as loud as any words.

21. I Started a Poem...

I started a poem trying to tell you.

I started a poem trying to ask you.

I started a poem, trying to mix the two.

To convey how,
while the ask was the same
the reasons were different.

I started a poem
seeking to expose all the meaning that lies
between the sentences on the page.

I struggle to find the words,
at least in a language I speak.

Too many broken sentences.
Written over and over again.
Never quite finding their proper place on the page.

So instead,

a very unlike me thing to do.

I'll hold my tongue.

www.ingramcontent.com/pod-product-compliance
Lightning Source LLC
Chambersburg PA
CBHW071237140726
47996CB00007B/2643